Orbiting EYES

The Science of **Artificial Satellites**

by Don Nardo

Content Adviser:
James Gerard, NASA Education Specialist,
Kennedy Space Center

Science Adviser:
Terrence E. Young Jr., M.Ed., M.L.S.,
Jefferson Parish (Louisiana) Public School System

Reading Adviser:
Rosemary G. Palmer, Ph.D., Department of Literacy,
College of Education, Boise State University

Compass Point Books • 151 Good Counsel Drive, P. O. Box 669 • Mankato, MN 56002-0669

Library of Congress Cataloging-in-Publication Data
Nardo, Don, 1947–
 Orbiting eyes : the science of artificial satellites / by Don Nardo.
  p. cm. — (Headline Science)
 Includes bibliographical references and index.
 ISBN 978-0-7565-4058-6 (library binding)
 1. Artificial satellites—Juvenile literature. I. Title. II. Series.
 TL796.N35 2009
 626.43'4—dc22   2008037572

Editor: Jennifer VanVoorst
Designers: Ellen Schofield and Ashlee Suker
Page Production: Ashlee Suker
Photo Researcher: Svetlana Zhurkin

Art Director: LuAnn Ascheman-Adams
Creative Director: Joe Ewest
Editorial Director: Nick Healy
Managing Editor: Catherine Neitge

Photographs ©: Cristi Matei/Shutterstock, cover (bottom); NASA and The Hubble Heritage Team (AURA/STScI),
cover (inset, left), 38; EUMETSAT, cover (inset, middle), 15; Sebastien Cote/iStockphoto, cover (inset, right), 29;
The Granger Collection, New York, 5; OFF/AFP/Getty Images, 7; Marilyn Moseley LaMantia, 8; NASA, 10, 11, 17,
21, 22, 39; NASA/Tim Terry, 12; AP Photo/IKONOS satellite image courtesy of GeoEye, 14; PhotoFritz/iStockphoto,
16; NASA Goddard Space Flight Center, 18; Jeff Schmaltz, MODIS Land Rapid Response Team, NASA GSFC, 19;
Jiann Jong Lim/iStockphoto, 24; Roberta Casaliggi/iStockphoto, 26; PhotoSky4t/Shutterstock, 27; Wojtek Kryczka/
iStockphoto, 28; AP Photo/Kyodo News, 31; Popperfoto/Getty Images, 32; AP Photo/GeoEye, 33; Photographer's
Choice/Erik Simonsen/Getty Images, 35; NASA, ESA, and The Hubble Heritage Team (STScI), 37; NASA Kennedy
Space Center, 41; NASA Jet Propulsion Laboratory, 42; John Woodworth/iStockphoto, 43.

Visit Compass Point Books on the Internet at *www.compasspointbooks.com*
or e-mail your request to *custserv@compasspointbooks.com*

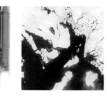

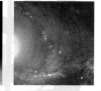

FIFTY YEARS AFTER SPUTNIK

Science Daily
October 5, 2007

In cosmic terms, half a century is a mere blink of an eyelid. But for mankind, much has happened in the 50 years since *Sputnik 1*, the first artificial satellite, was launched by the Soviet Union on 4 October 1957.

Despite being little more than a sphere of metal that let out radio-frequency beeps, *Sputnik 1* triggered a thrilling space race that led to astronauts soon orbiting the earth and walking on the moon before the 1960s were out. Since then, spacecraft have visited planets, flown past comets and even landed on an asteroid.

The Soviet Union's launch of the first satellite in 1957 took the rest of the world, including the United States, by surprise. It probably should not have. The Soviets had announced two years before that they were planning to launch a satellite. The United States had begun serious work on satellites at the same time. But no one expected the Soviets to succeed so quickly. That success both surprised and irritated American scientists and leaders. The result was the famous "space race" between the United States and the Soviet Union. The Americans launched their first satellite, *Explorer 1,* in 1958. They went on to win the race by putting a man on the moon in 1969.

The front page of The New York Times *announced the Soviet Union's launch of* Sputnik 1, *the first satellite;* Sputnik *means "traveling companion" in Russian.*

KEEPING CURRENT

News changes every minute, and readers need access to the latest information to keep current. Here are a few key search terms to help you locate up-to-the-minute satellite headlines:

anti-satellite weapons (ASATs)

BASIC program

GeoEye

GPS satellites

International Space Station

James Webb Space Telescope

National Aeronautics and Space Administration (NASA)

PLANETS, SATELLITES, AND ORBITS

To appreciate the significance of these early scientific achievements, one must consider what goes into launching satellites. A satellite is an object that moves around a planet or other cosmic body. Some satellites are natural. For example, the planets Earth, Venus, and Mars are natural satellites of their central star, the sun. The moon is Earth's single natural satellite. Mars has two natural satellites, and the giant planets Jupiter, Saturn, and Uranus have dozens each.

In contrast, *Sputnik 1* and *Explorer 1* were manufactured and launched by humans. Such devices are referred to as artificial satellites. These artificial satellites are put into space for a wide range of purposes. Some study Earth's surface, the moon, the planets, and the stars. Others are used for weather observations or communications. Still others spy on the competitors and enemies of those countries that

THE FIRST SATELLITE

By today's standards, *Sputnik 1* was both small and simple. It was a 23-inch (58-centimeter), 184-pound (83-kilogram) metal ball containing a thermometer, a radio transmitter, and a battery to power the instruments. It also had four antennas, which transmitted short beeps to Earth. The tone of the beeps changed based on the thermometer readings. Launched on October 4, 1957, *Sputnik 1* circled Earth once every 96 minutes and could be seen passing overhead at dawn and in the evening. After 92 days in orbit, gravity took over, and the satellite burned up in Earth's atmosphere.

launch them.

In order to accomplish those goals, all satellites are equipped with a variety of instruments, called the payload. These instruments vary according to the purpose of the satellite, but all satellites have some equipment in common. All satellites have a power source, such as solar panels, and a battery to store the power. This power is used to operate the instruments. Satellites have an onboard computer that monitors and controls the various systems. They also have a radio transmitter and receiver so that they can send and receive information to and from the ground control team. Satellites are also equipped with a control system that allows their path to be adjusted as needed by people on Earth.

The path a satellite follows around Earth or another cosmic body is called its orbit. Satellites can orbit a central body in many different ways. One is called synchronous orbit. An Earth satellite is in synchronous orbit if it moves at the same speed that the planet rotates on its axis. (Earth spins on its axis once each day.) Such an object will always stay parked, so to speak, above the same spot on Earth's surface. So it will appear to remain stationary in the sky, even though it is moving very fast. For that reason, synchronous orbits are also called stationary orbits. They are also called geosynchronous or geostationary orbits, because the orbits are fixed with regard to Earth—*geo* in Latin.

In contrast, many satellites do not move at the same speed that Earth spins. Their orbits are said to be asynchronous. Such a satellite will pass over many areas of the planet's surface.

Satellites are placed into orbit at various altitudes based on their uses. And they orbit the planet at various rates. For example, satellites that operate in low Earth orbit—from

Because the planets in our solar system all orbit a central body, the sun, they are all satellites. Earth takes a year to complete its orbit around the sun; closer planets take less time, and more distant planets take longer.

NOW YOU KNOW

Many satellites move in elliptical—oval-shaped—orbits. That means that at times a satellite is closer to Earth's surface than at other times. The farthest point in its orbit is called the apogee. The closest point is the perigee.

100 to 1,240 miles (161 to 1,996 kilometers) above Earth—take about 90 minutes to circle the planet. Satellites that are much higher in the sky take longer to complete their paths. Those satellites in geosynchronous orbit—22,240 miles (35,584 km) up—match Earth's rotation. Their orbital period is a full 24 hours.

A SPECIAL BALANCE

Whatever orbit a satellite has, getting it into that orbit in the first place is no easy task. This is mainly because Earth's powerful gravity exerts a very strong pull on surface objects, including rocks, cars, and people. Gravity also pulls on satellites.

SATELLITE ORBIT TYPES

Name	Altitude	Orbital Period	Applications
Low Earth Orbit	100–1,240 miles (161–1,996 km)	~90 minutes	Earth observation, astronomical observatories
Medium Earth Orbit	>1,240–<22,240 miles (>1,996–<35,584 km)	2–<24 hours	navigation, communications
Geosynchronous Orbit	22,240 miles (35,584 km)	24 hours	weather, communications
High Earth Orbit	>22,240 miles (>35,584 km)	>24 hours	astronomical observatories

Source: NASA

To achieve orbit and become a satellite, an object must resist Earth's gravity and attain what scientists call orbital velocity. This is the speed at which the object needs to travel in order to achieve a balance between gravity's pull on the object and the object's forward motion. If the object moves slower than orbital velocity, gravity will win out, and the object will fall back to Earth. On the other hand, if the object moves faster than orbital velocity, it will escape the planet's gravity and fly off into space. In that case, it will not be a satellite, but rather an interplanetary spacecraft. Only when the two forces balance and cancel each other out does the object achieve and remain in orbit.

The orbital velocity of a satellite depends on that object's distance from Earth or whatever cosmic body it will

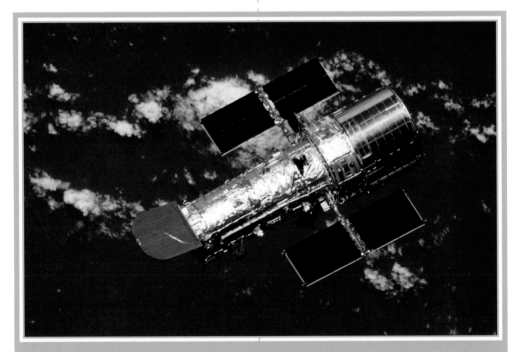

The Hubble Space Telescope is a satellite that orbits Earth 375 miles (604 km) above the planet's surface; it looks outward into space to help scientists learn about the universe.

be orbiting. The nearer the satellite is to the body it orbits, the faster it must move to cancel out gravity and stay in orbit. Take the example of the moon, a natural satellite of Earth. At a distance of about 240,000 miles (386,400 km) from Earth, the moon's orbital velocity is roughly 2,300 miles (3,703 km) per hour. In contrast, most artificial satellites orbit much closer to Earth. As a result, they must move a great deal faster. At a height of 150 miles (241 km) above the planet's surface, a satellite must travel about 17,000 mph (27,370 kph) to remain in orbit.

A MODERN REVOLUTION

The American and Soviet scientists who sought to launch the first satellites faced a daunting challenge. To send them into near-Earth orbit, the satellites had to achieve enormous speeds. Ordinary airplanes, even jets, were not nearly fast enough.

The only devices that seemed capable of this task were rocket engines. The Chinese had invented the first rockets in the 13th century. They had

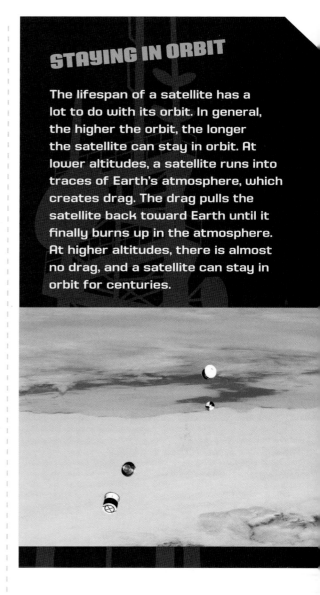

STAYING IN ORBIT

The lifespan of a satellite has a lot to do with its orbit. In general, the higher the orbit, the longer the satellite can stay in orbit. At lower altitudes, a satellite runs into traces of Earth's atmosphere, which creates drag. The drag pulls the satellite back toward Earth until it finally burns up in the atmosphere. At higher altitudes, there is almost no drag, and a satellite can stay in orbit for centuries.

used these small, primitive devices to make noise and smoke to scare enemies in wartime. In 1903, Russian scientist Konstantin Tsiolkovsky

Rockets such as the Boeing Delta IV are used to launch satellites into space; the satellites travel atop the rocket's nose cone.

proposed using rockets to launch objects into space. Both Russian and American experiments followed. In 1937, American researcher Robert Goddard sent a rocket hurtling to a height of 9,000 feet (2,745 meters)—almost two miles (three km). During and after World War II, rocket research became still more advanced. Steady improvements led to the *Sputnik* 1 and *Explorer* 1 launches in the late 1950s.

Since that time, the United States, the Soviet Union—now Russia—and other nations have launched thousands of artificial satellites. France sent its first satellite into orbit in 1965. Australia did the same two years later, and the list of countries with satellite programs quickly expanded. Today there are more than 3,000 satellites in orbit owned by more than 40 countries worldwide.

These orbiting eyes are among the most influential of all human inventions. In only a few decades they have revolutionized the way people live, communicate, learn, and do business. ◤

NASA ANNOUNCES NEW WEATHER SATELLITE LAUNCH DATE

NASA
May 18, 2006

NASA announced the launch date for a weather satellite that will provide timely environmental information to meteorologists and the public. The *Geostationary Operational Environmental Satellite-N*, known as *GOES-N*, ... joins a system of weather satellites that graphically display the intensity, path and size of storms. Early warning about severe weather enhances the public's ability to take shelter and protect property.

Of the more than 3,000 satellites in orbit today, the vast majority of them have their "eyes" focused on Earth. Among them are weather satellites. In the past half-century, weather satellites have revolutionized weather forecasting. They have given meteorologists—scientists who study the weather—the ability to make long-range and mostly reliable forecasts.

Weather satellites show hurricanes forming in the oceans. They monitor the exact paths of these monster storms, giving advance warning to cities in those paths. Weather satellites also track thunderstorms and snowstorms over land. They help meteorologists predict rain and snowfall amounts with greater accuracy. Weather satellites also monitor large fires and the effects of air pollution on forests. In addition, they measure the movements of dust storms, the drift of volcanic ash falls, the patterns

A satellite image from October 2007 showed smoke rising from fires near Barrett Reservoir outside San Diego, California.

A satellite image from 2004 showed dust from Africa's Sahara Desert spreading west across the Atlantic Ocean.

and intensity of city lights, and much more. All of this information has greatly improved the day-to-day lives of ordinary people.

Weather satellites are just one kind of Earth observation satellite. Other similar orbiters study gases in the atmosphere or measure changes in the planet's gravity and magnetic field. Others take detailed photos of Earth's surface. These are used to make accurate maps and to aid in planning large-scale uses of natural resources. All Earth observation satellites do valuable scientific research, so they are often referred to as scientific research satellites. They vary considerably in size. Some are only a few feet across, while others are space stations more than 100 feet (30 m) long. Like all satellites, they are equipped with special electronic receivers and transmitters. The electronic receivers gather instructions beamed by scientists on Earth. These instructions are processed by an onboard computer, which then orders cameras and other instruments to perform various tasks. Finally the radio transmitter sends the data the instruments have gathered back to receivers on Earth.

Satellite dishes point skyward to transmit and receive radio signals from space.

STEADY ADVANCES IN WEATHER RESEARCH

Not surprisingly, the first research satellites were very small and fairly simple by today's standards. The first successful weather satellite was *TIROS 1,* launched by the newly formed National Aeronautics and Space Administration (NASA) in 1960. Weighing 270 pounds (122 kilograms), it was powered by 9,200 attached solar cells. The cells converted sunlight to electricity, which was used to power two television cameras. These cameras took more than 22,000 images of clouds and other weather phenomena.

Today new generations of weather satellites orbit Earth. Among the most effective and reliable are the U.S.-launched GOES orbiters. GOES stands for Geostationary Operational Environmental Satellite. The term geostationary is revealing. Like most weather satellites, those in the GOES series move in synchronous—stationary—Earth orbits. That allows them to stay above target areas on Earth and monitor changes on a long-term basis. Four GOES satellites—numbers 9, 10, 11, and 12—are presently in orbit, although only *GOES-10* and *GOES-11* are fully operational. These satellites carry complex cameras, X-ray and heat sensors, and other advanced instruments for collecting weather-

NASA's TIROS 1 satellite during its testing phase in December 1960

related data.

Many other weather satellites currently orbit Earth. Among them are four operated by the National Oceanic and Atmospheric Administration. EUMETSAT, a European organization, oversees four weather satellites, and Russia, Japan, India, and China all have weather satellites working around the clock. This large collection of orbiting devices keeps constant track of weather changes in every part of the globe.

MAPPING THE PLANET

Meanwhile, other scientific research satellites regularly collect vast amounts of data about the planet. Among the most successful are the U.S. Landsat orbit-

ers. Seven Landsats were launched between 1972 and 1999. Their mission is to take detailed photos of Earth's surface. So far they have collected millions of images, many of superb quality. These have been used to produce accurate maps of every square

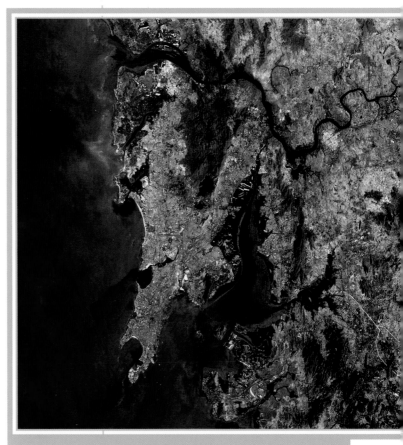

An image of the Mumbai, India, harbor was captured by the Landsat 7 satellite.

inch of the planet's landmasses. The Landsats' images have also helped in planning large-scale agricultural programs. In addition, big forestry, logging, and road-building projects have benefited from the Landsat photos.

In 1999, the same year that *Landsat 7* reached orbit, an American company, GeoEye, launched *IKONOS*. The name comes from a Greek word meaning "image." This is fitting because *IKONOS* takes photos of hundreds of square miles of Earth's surface each day. Its images are more detailed than those of the Landsats—*IKONOS* can see surface objects as small as 3 feet (90 cm) across. Incredibly, the cameras aboard its most recent orbiter—*GeoEye-1*—can make out objects smaller than half that size. GeoEye's satellites provide map images to Web search engines such as Microsoft, Yahoo!, and Google.

Other recently launched

CIRCLING THE POLES

Many satellites that survey the planet's surface travel in a polar orbit. This means that these satellites orbit the planet in a north-south direction rather than in the more common east-west direction. Polar orbits are useful for viewing the planet's surface. As a satellite orbits around the poles, Earth spins beneath it in the opposite direction. By making slight, regular changes to the satellite's path, over time a satellite in polar orbit can eventually scan the entire planet.

observation satellites are presently collecting other types of scientific data. *Jason 1*, for example, is a joint mission of the United States and France. It was launched in 2001 to study the Earth's oceans. *Jason 1* measures the speed of ocean currents and wind speeds at the water's surface. In March 2002, NASA launched twin GRACE satellites, which stands for Gravity Recovery and Climate Experiment. The GRACE satellites map variations in Earth's gravity. They also study shifts in the planet's crust caused by earthquakes.

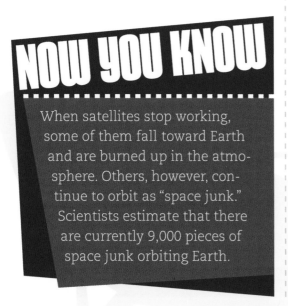

NOW YOU KNOW

When satellites stop working, some of them fall toward Earth and are burned up in the atmosphere. Others, however, continue to orbit as "space junk." Scientists estimate that there are currently 9,000 pieces of space junk orbiting Earth.

ORBITING SCIENCE LABS

The largest of the scientific research satellites are the orbiting space stations. They need to be large because the scientists who are collecting the data are not doing so remotely—they are living and working inside the satellites themselves.

The first space station to make it into orbit was the Soviet *Salyut 1*, launched in 1971. The United States followed two years later with the 100-ton (91-metric-ton) *Skylab*. Like the instruments on standard weather satellites, the astronauts aboard *Skylab* monitored Earth's weather patterns. They also studied the planet's landmasses and oceans. And in the space station's onboard science lab, they performed experiments having to do with the human body's response to a weightless environment.

The largest satellite ever to orbit Earth is the International Space Station (ISS). It is a joint project of the United States, Russia, Japan, Canada, and several European nations. The ISS operates in low Earth orbit at an

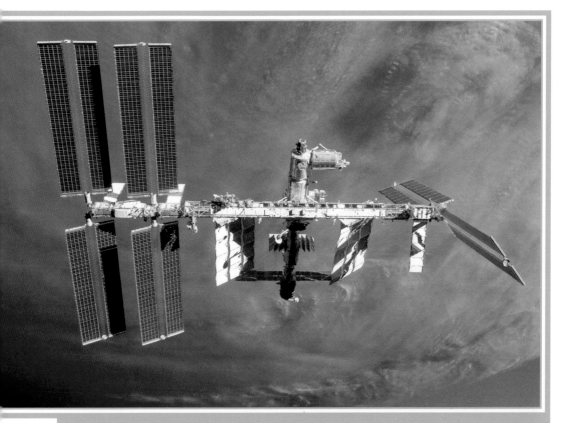

The International Space Station was photographed in February 2008 by a crew member on the space shuttle Atlantis.

altitude of 220 miles (354 km) above the planet. Inside, the space station is larger than a three-bedroom house. Because of its large size and low altitude, it can be seen from the ground with the naked eye.

The first section of the space station reached orbit in 1998. A few new sections are added each year, with completion scheduled for 2010. When complete, the ISS will have 14 sections and be home to six astronauts and scientists. Today the ISS is home to three astronauts at a time. Since November 2002, when the first crew arrived on the ISS, it has been continuously inhabited. Seventeen teams of scientists have performed science experiments to learn more about how humans can survive in space. The crews have also made important observations of Earth, including taking photos of Hurricane Ike in September 2008.

The ISS, the GRACE and GOES orbiters, and other similar satellites stand at the forefront of modern scientific research. They continue to provide new insights into the way the world works, making human society safer, more efficient, and more able to plan for the future.

In September 2008, a crew member on board the International Space Station photographed Hurricane Ike as the storm's eye swirled over the island of Cuba.

NEWEST GPS SPACECRAFT SUCCESSFULLY SOARS INTO ORBIT

Justin Ray
Spaceflight Now
March 20, 2004

As the 50th Global Positioning System satellite rose to space Saturday, it celebrated the man who championed the concept of orbiting spacecraft serving as "lighthouses in the sky" to guide mankind with precision navigation information. ... In a lasting tribute that will circle 11,000 miles above the planet, a famous quote by [GPS pioneer Ivan] Getting, "Lighthouses in the Sky, Serving All Mankind," was inscribed on the *GPS 2R-11* spacecraft. ... Riding atop a three-stage Boeing Delta 2 rocket, the craft was delivered into a temporary elliptical orbit stretching from 100 miles above Earth at the closest spot to nearly 11,000 miles at apogee.

Physicist and electrical engineer Ivan Getting was not the only person who long ago foresaw the direct use of satellite signals by everyday people. The famous science fiction writer Arthur C. Clarke was another. He was the first person to describe the idea of a communications satellite. In February 1945, he wrote in the magazine *Wireless World:*

An "artificial satellite" at the correct distance from the earth would remain stationary above the same spot and would be within optical range of nearly half the earth's surface. Three [such orbiting] stations, 120 degrees apart in the correct orbit, could give [communications] coverage to the entire planet.

People around the world rely on satellites to communicate with each other, receive broadcast information, and find their way around.

The dreams of both men eventually became reality. Today people regularly use satellite information to get directions to new locations. They watch television shows and answer phone calls provided by communications satellites. These orbiting devices allow people to stay in touch with other individuals. They also make it possible to keep up with what is happening all around the world.

A WIDE VARIETY OF PRACTICAL USES

The idea of using satellites for navigation originated with military research. In the 1950s, Ivan Getting developed a method for pinpointing the precise locations of targets for Army missiles. In time, he realized that a similar system could be used to help ordinary people. A person could use satellite signals to find a chosen destination or to keep from getting lost. In other words, these satellites could aid in navigation.

Getting's research led to the development of the Global Positioning System (GPS). This system consists of a network of 24 satellites, plus three extras that can be activated in case of failure. They provide data that locate the exact positions of objects on Earth.

GPS satellites are sensitive measuring devices. Each contains an extremely accurate, reliable clock. Each also features a transmitter. Using its transmitter, each of a group of four of the orbiters sends out a constant electronic signal. The four signals

NOW YOU KNOW

At present, GPS is the only fully operational navigational satellite system in the world. It was developed by the U.S. Department of Defense. It is currently run by the U.S. Air Force at a cost of about $750 million per year. Other nations are working on similar systems. Among them are Russia, China, India, and several European countries.

Most vehicles equipped with GPS receivers feature mapping software that helps drivers identify their location and find the best route to their destinations.

travel to a receiver on Earth. That receiver can be in a car, ship, mobile telephone, wristwatch, or other piece of equipment.

Next, a small computer in the receiver goes to work. In a split second it calculates the distances between the receiver and each satellite. Knowing these figures, the computer easily determines the receiver's exact posi-

tion by applying simple math. The system is amazingly accurate. According to science reporter Justin Ray, "time can be figured to less than a millionth of a second, velocity [speed] to within a fraction of a mile per hour, and location to within a few feet."

Such pinpoint accuracy makes GPS ideal for a wide variety of practical uses. Ships at sea find navigating easier and more precise than ever before. It also aids emergency services and rescue teams in locating sick people and accident victims. GPS makes the work of surveyors and mapmakers more accurate. And wildlife researchers use it to track migrating animals that have been implanted with tiny tracking devices.

CONNECTING OUR WORLD

Communications satellites also send signals to receivers on Earth. The difference is that these orbiters act as

Many outdoors enthusiasts carry GPS receivers to keep them from getting lost in the wilderness.

relay stations. A ground station sends a radio, TV, or telephone signal to a satellite. The orbiter then relays the signal to a second station.

Often these stations are thousands of miles apart. That means that people in one country can contact people in faraway countries. For instance, someone in Chicago can speak to a friend in Paris simply by dialing a cell phone. Soccer fans in the United States can watch a European match live. Before the birth of satellites, such feats were possible only with long cables to carry the signals. Today the signals race through the air and bounce off satellites.

The first successful satellite created primarily for communications was *Telstar 1*. Launched in July 1962, it was a joint project of AT&T, Bell Telephone Laboratories, NASA, and some British and French companies. The device was a mere 35 inches (89 centimeters) across and weighed 170 pounds (77 kg). Many more Telstars were launched over the years. The latest, *Telstar 18*, began operating in 2004. Other successful communications satellites or satellite systems have included Syncom, TELKOM, Westar, and SATCOM.

Mobile phones send signals to radio towers, which then transmit the communication to satellites.

Because satellite dishes need to be able to transmit data to and receive data from orbiting satellites, they must be placed with a clear view of the sky.

These and other satellites have carried billions of phone conversations and thousands of TV programs around the world. In some ways this has brought many diverse peoples and societies together, which in turn has promoted increased understanding among them. Arthur C. Clarke saw this human dimension as the most important aspect of satellites. When asked, shortly before he died, to name the greatest invention of the 20th century, he chose the communications satellite. "I'm very proud," he said, "to have played a part in changing history and in fact changing the whole human family, because we are now essentially one family, whether we like it or not."

U.S. PURSUING NEW SPY SATELLITE PROGRAM

CBS News
November 30, 2007

The U.S. is pursuing a multibillion-dollar program to develop the next generation of spy satellites. ... The new system, known as BASIC, would be launched by 2011 and is expected to cost $2 billion to $4 billion, according to U.S. officials familiar with the program. ... Photo reconnaissance (spy) satellites are used to gather visual information from space about adversarial (enemy) governments and terror groups, such as construction at suspected nuclear sites or militant training camps.

The upcoming BASIC program is only the latest in a long line of spy satellite programs. The official term for these orbiters is reconnaissance satellites. A reconnaissance satellite is one used for military purposes. By far the most important of these purposes is to gather information about other countries seen as enemies or potential enemies. That information, which is usually related to war-making abilities, is called intelligence. Military officials say that such intelligence-gathering is mainly defensive in nature. That is, they feel they need to know about military developments in other nations in order to protect the U.S. homeland from possible attack.

Other countries use the same argument to justify their own spy satellites. China, Russia, France, and the United Kingdom all have spy satellites in orbit. So do Germany, Israel, Japan, and South Korea, among others.

In 2007, Japan launched its fourth spy satellite into orbit; it will be used, among other things, to monitor North Korea's nuclear program.

COLD WAR SPY SATELLITES

Though many nations now have military satellites, the United States and the former Soviet Union pioneered these devices. In the 1950s, the two superpowers were engaged in the so-called "Cold War." Neither attacked the other, but each feared the other might do so. In particular, leaders on both sides worried that nuclear weapons might be used. It was important, therefore, to have up-to-date information about the enemy's military capabilities. Such information was often gathered by high-flying airplanes. But secret flights over enemy territory were risky. The spy planes might be shot down, and surviving pilots might fall into enemy hands.

The U.S. military wanted to avoid such incidents. So military leaders decided to try a bold new approach—reconnaissance satellites. Such devices, scientists told them, could gather the necessary intelligence, and they would fly so high that they could not be shot down. In March 1955, top U.S. officials secretly ordered

SPYING ON THE SOVIETS

The U.S. spy satellite program paid off in 1962 when satellites took photos of Soviet missiles on the island of Cuba. Because Cuba is so close to Florida, the U.S. government viewed the missiles' presence as a threat to U.S. security. In the ensuing "Cuban Missile Crisis," President John F. Kennedy demanded that the Soviets remove the missiles. And fearing a U.S. military response, they did so.

the development of a military satellite program. Its goal was to create an orbiter that would observe selected areas of Earth's surface "to determine the status of a potential enemy's war-making capability."

Most of what is known about the military use of satellites is historical. Information on spy satellites that existed before 1972 is more or less available. Details of recent programs, however, are hard to come by. Magnum, Trumpet, Mercury, and MENTOR are all U.S. spy satellite programs that existed in the 1990s and into the 2000s. But besides their names, very little is known about these and current spy satellites. Not surprisingly, the military keeps such information a closely guarded secret.

Satellites in these programs likely use a variety of high-tech electronic tools to gather data, much like the instruments used by Earth observation satellites. High-resolution cameras on

A satellite image of the seat of U.S. government—Washington, D.C.'s Capitol Hill

spy satellites reportedly can capture images of objects on Earth as small as 3.9 inches (9.9 cm) across. Heat sensors can detect the radiation given off by factories, homes, vehicles, and even individual people.

Slightly more is known about the Satellite Data System. It consists of a series of communications satellites run by the military. The SDS orbiters relay electronic information from spy satellites to ground stations. Several of these satellites are thought to have been launched by a space shuttle, and the most recent is thought to have been put into orbit in December 2007.

NOW YOU KNOW

Reconnaissance satellites built by other countries also operate mostly in secret. Among the most successful of these were the orbiters in Russia's Zenit program. U.S. authorities believe that more than 500 Zenits were launched from the 1960s to the 1990s.

BATTLEFIELD SPACE

The United Sates, Russia, and China operate still other top-secret space programs involving satellites. They are generally referred to as ASATs, which stands for anti-satellite weapons. As the name suggests, their purpose is to destroy enemy satellites. The exact way they work has not been revealed. But some are reportedly designed to send missiles or other high-speed devices crashing into target satellites, smashing them to bits. In January 2007, China successfully tested this sort of ASAT on one of its own weather satellites. Scientists in the United States have also experimented with laser beams to shoot down satellites. Their degree of success is unclear.

Many people find the development of such space weapons unsettling. They worry that space might someday become a battlefield similar to that seen in movies like *Star Wars*. Others view these devices as necessary to

An unidentified military intelligence satellite orbits Earth; spy satellites gather ground data using many of the same tools as weather and Earth observation satellites.

national security. Throughout history, they say, every new weapon has inspired the creation of counter-measures. This debate has only just begun. There is little doubt that military satellites and ASATs will remain facts of life for a long time to come. ▧

35

HUBBLE FINDS LARGE SAMPLE OF VERY DISTANT GALAXIES

Spaceflight Now
August 4, 2008

New Hubble Space Telescope observations of six spectacular galaxy clusters ... have given significant insights into the early stages of the universe. Scientists have found the largest sample of very distant galaxies seen to date. ... [The] 10 candidates [are] believed to lie about 13 billion light years away ... which means that the light gathered was emitted by the stars when the universe was still very young—a mere 700 million years old.

Most Earth-orbiting satellites look down at Earth, gathering data about our planet and relaying it to scientists, citizens, and soldiers on the ground. But there are some satellites that look elsewhere. Revealing distant galaxies is only one of the many extraordinary achievements of the Hubble Space Telescope, which orbits Earth but looks to the stars.

Orbiting Earth at a height of 375 miles (604 km), the Hubble surveys the heavens 24 hours a day. It has photographed the sun, planets, and planetary moons. It has also witnessed the birth and death of stars. It has shown the breakup of comets and peered into deep space where it has found new galaxies, each a massive collection of billions of stars.

NASA's Hubble Space Telescope captured an image of two spiral galaxies, NGC 2207 and IC 2163, nearly colliding as they passed by one another.

BEYOND THE ATMOSPHERE

Hubble's successes have made it one of the most valuable satellites ever launched into orbit. Because it aids the science of astronomy, experts classify it as an astronomical satellite. Hubble and other satellites that study cosmic bodies beyond Earth are also called space observatories.

Most of the cosmic objects that Hubble sees are also visible from Earth's surface. But images of them in ground-based telescopes have limited detail and quality. This is because

In 2004, the Hubble Space Telescope captured an image of an unusual phenomenon called a light echo. Light from a star that erupted in 2002 passed through a cloud of dust surrounding the star; the light "echoed" off the dust and then traveled to Earth.

these telescopes must see through the planet's atmosphere. That miles-thick blanket of air both absorbs and scatters rays of light that pass through it. It distorts images of stars, planets, and other cosmic objects seen through Earth-bound telescopes.

Astronomical satellites eliminate this problem by placing observation devices beyond the atmosphere. Some, like Hubble, orbit Earth. Others orbit the sun, moon, and several of the planets.

ORBITING OBSERVATORIES

Of the many astronomical observatories placed in Earth orbit, the Hubble Space Telescope was the first large-scale one. At 44 feet (13 m) long and 14 feet (4 m) across, it is about the size of a school bus. Since its launch in April 1990, the telescope has captured thousands of spectacular images of various aspects of the universe. Among them are photos of galaxies too distant and faint for ground-based telescopes to detect. Hubble has also collected data proving the existence of

The Hubble Space Telescope is in an orbit that allows it to be serviced by astronauts.

black holes. These are objects so dense that their enormous gravities will not allow anything, even light, to escape. In addition, the orbiting telescope has examined vast clouds of gas floating in deep space. In 1994, it captured dazzling images of a comet, Shoemaker-Levy 9, crashing into Jupiter.

Hubble is not the only Earth-orbiting satellite equipped with an observatory for studying the heavens. In July 1999, NASA launched the Chandra X-ray Observatory. A number of cosmic bodies give off X-rays. Because Earth's atmosphere readily absorbs these rays, they are mostly invisible to ground-based instruments. Orbiting high above the atmosphere, Chandra has detected thousands of X-ray sources. Among them are bursts of X-rays given off when the immense gravities of black holes rip apart cosmic gases. Thus, Chandra has provided further proof of the existence of black holes.

NASA launched another orbiting observatory in August 2003. Called the Spitzer Space Telescope, this highly sensitive instrument detects distant objects by measuring the heat they give off.

NASA plans to launch even more advanced observatories into orbit in the near future. Among these is the eagerly awaited James Webb Space Telescope. Scheduled to begin surveying the universe in 2013, it will be sent into orbit at a height of 940,000 miles (1.5 million km). From this position, it will orbit the sun, not Earth. The telescope will be able to observe the most distant objects in the universe—those well beyond the reach of the Hubble. It will search for light from the first stars and galaxies that formed after the Big Bang and help scientists understand the formation of stars and planets and the origins of life.

EYES BEYOND EARTH

NASA and some foreign space agencies have also sent satellite astronomical observatories far beyond Earth orbit to observe other planets. In May 1971, NASA's *Mariner 9* arrived at Mars and became the first satellite ever to

Technicians made final checks of Mariner 9 before its 1971 liftoff and six-month-long trip to Mars.

orbit another planet. *Mariner 9*'s photos revealed several craters and some enormous volcanoes on the red planet. That November, two Soviet satellites—*Mars 2* and *Mars 3*—reached Mars and began recording valuable data.

Far beyond Mars lie the giant planets Jupiter and Saturn. Man-made spacecraft had flown past these bodies in the 1970s and 1980s. However, in order to conduct long-term studies, scientists needed to have observatories in orbit around them. The first satellite to orbit Jupiter was *Galileo*, named for the famous 17th century Italian astronomer. Beginning in 1995, *Galileo* collected reams of data on Jupiter's atmosphere, magnetic field, and moons.

In 2004, NASA's *Cassini* satellite went into orbit around Saturn. It has provided important information about that planet's famous rings and its many moons. (At last count, there are 52, many of which *Cassini* discovered.) For instance, *Cassini* revealed that the icy moon Enceladus has giant water geysers erupting from its surface.

An image taken by NASA's Cassini satellite showed, by color, the variation in composition of Saturn's rings.

Some of the frozen water escapes from the moon, and Saturn's gravity draws the floating ice crystals in to merge with and expand its gigantic ring system. The *Cassini* satellite took photos that show that the few broad rings visible from Earth are made up of many thousands of tiny "ringlets."

With more than 3,000 active satellites in orbit, there's no question that satellites are a crucial part of our lives. Whether they observe Earth for science, business, or defense—or even if they observe the heavens—they are advancing the way we live and learn, one launch at a time.

Roofs in Fez, Morocco, and throughout the world are dotted with satellite dishes, which provide communications in the form of telephone, Internet, television, GPS, and radio service.

1903
Russian scientist Konstantin Tsiolkovsky proposes using rockets to launch objects into space

1945
Noted writer Arthur C. Clarke predicts the advent of communications satellites

1946
Princeton University scientist Lyman Spitzer Jr. proposes building a space telescope

1955
The U.S. military begins developing a satellite to gather information about its enemies

1957
The Soviet Union launches *Sputnik 1*, the first artificial satellite

1958
The United States launches its first satellite, *Explorer 1*

1959
The United States launches the first weather satellite— *Vanguard II*

1962
The United States launches the first successful communications satellite, *Telstar 1*

1965
France launches its first satellite

1971
Mariner 9, launched by the United States, reaches Mars and becomes the first satellite to orbit another planet; the Soviets launch the first space station—*Salyut 1*—into orbit around Earth

1990
The Hubble Space Telescope begins orbiting Earth and taking photos of the universe

2001
Jason 1, a satellite sponsored by the United States and France, begins studying Earth's oceans

2003
The U.S. Spitzer Space Telescope is launched into orbit

2004
NASA's *Cassini* satellite goes into orbit around the planet Saturn

2008
GeoEye, an American company, launches its *GeoEye-1* satellite, which can see objects as small as 16 inches (41 cm)

2013
Proposed date for the launch of the James Webb Space Telescope

Timeline

GLOSSARY

anti-satellite weapons (ASATs)
devices designed to cripple or destroy
orbiting satellites

apogee
farthest point in a satellite's orbit

astronomical satellite
satellite designed to study cosmic bodies
lying beyond Earth

asynchronous orbit
orbit in which a satellite passes over
many areas of the planet below

cosmic
having to do with outer space, the
universe, or the heavens

elliptical
oval-shaped

intelligence
information gathered about an enemy's
war-making abilities

meteorologist
scientist who studies the weather

orbit
path taken by a satellite around a planet
or other cosmic body

orbital velocity
speed an object needs to attain in order
to go into orbit

perigee
closest point in a satellite's orbit

radiation
microscopic particles given off
by unstable atoms and various
nuclear materials

reconnaissance satellite
military satellite used for spying

satellite
object that moves around a planet or
other cosmic body

solar system
sun and all the planets, moons, comets,
and other objects moving around it

synchronous orbit
orbit in which a satellite remains always
above a certain spot on the planet

FURTHER RESOURCES

ON THE WEB

For more information on this topic, use FactHound.

1. Go to *www.facthound.com*
2. Choose your grade level.
3. Begin your search.

This book's ID number is 9780756540586

FactHound will find the best sites for you.

FURTHER READING

Byers, Ann. *Communications Satellites*. New York: Rosen Central, 2003.

Flint, David. *The Satellite Atlas*. North Mankato, Minn.: Chrysalis Education, 2003.

Johnson, Rebecca L. *Satellites*. Minneapolis: Lerner Publications, 2006.

Miller, Ron. *Satellites*. Minneapolis: Twenty-First Century Books, 2008.

Wolny, Philip. *Weapons Satellites*. New York: Rosen Publishing Group, 2003.

LOOK FOR OTHER BOOKS IN THIS SERIES:

Climate Crisis: The Science of Global Warming

Collapse!: The Science of Structural Engineering Failures

Cure Quest: The Science of Stem Cell Research

Feel the G's: The Science of Gravity and G-Forces

Goodbye, Gasoline: The Science of Fuel Cells

Great Shakes: The Science of Earthquakes

Out of Control: The Science of Wildfires

Rise of the Thinking Machines: The Science of Robots

Storm Surge: The Science of Hurricanes

SOURCE NOTES

Chapter 1: "Fifty Years After *Sputnik*." *Science Daily*. 5 Oct. 2007. 15 Oct. 2008. www.sciencedaily.com/releases/2007/10/071003081901.htm

Chapter 2: "NASA Announces New Weather Satellite Launch Date." NASA. 18 May 2006. 15 Oct. 2008. www.nasa.gov/mission_pages/goes-n/media/HQ_M06088-GOES-N_update.html

Chapter 3: Justin Ray. "Newest GPS Spacecraft Successfully Soars into Orbit." *Spaceflight Now*. 20 March 2004. 15 Oct. 2008. www.spaceflightnow.com/delta/d303

Chapter 4: "U.S. Pursuing New Spy Satellite Program." CBS News. 30 Nov. 2007. 15 Oct. 2008. www.cbsnews.com/stories/2007/11/30/tech/main3561086.shtml

Chapter 5: "Hubble Finds Large Sample of Very Distant Galaxies." *Spaceflight Now*. 4 Aug. 2008. 15 Oct. 2008. www.spaceflightnow.com/news/n0808/04hubble

ABOUT THE AUTHOR

In addition to his numerous acclaimed volumes on ancient civilizations, historian Don Nardo has published several studies of modern scientific discoveries and phenomena. Nardo lives with his wife, Christine, in Massachusetts.

INDEX